D1647770

Bless
the
Children

Poems in the Spirit of Childhood

Bette Milleson James

Illuminations by Pamela Martin McCarville

Blueline Publishing LLC
Denver, Colorado

Bless the Children
Poems in the Spirit of Childhood

Copyright©2008 by Bette Milleson James

Designed by Pamela Martin McCarville

All rights reserved,
including the right of reproduction
in whole or in part in any form.

"*Snow Day*" was previously published in *Colorado Cravings*.

Blueline
PUBLISHING

Blueline Publishing LLC
Denver, Colorado
www.bluelinepub.com

Printed by R. R. Donnelley in Mexico

ISBN 978-0-9776906-3-3

Acknowledgments

After decades of teaching English to high school juniors and seniors, I found myself in a position to accept my own advice to those with writer's block: Begin. And in beginning this project, I found myself inspired by those young people and children who have passed through my life. Some are students, some are my own, some are grandchildren or others in the family, some are friends; all are a part of this little volume.

So it is that I owe loving gratitude to the family that has shared and enriched my life through the years: To my husband, Don; to my children, Mark, Myrna, and Karen; to their wisely chosen spouses, Elizabeth, Wooga, and Paul; and to the beloved generation of most promising grandchildren, Hanna, Madalyn, Jack, and Sam (four siblings who show us daily the perfection of each child of the universe), and Udo (the perfect little Korean boy who shows us daily the joyous outcome of the decision to adopt). In addition, thanks to Kellie and Kylie, and to Kelsey and Carman, two of the pairs of girls who have graced my life, for letting me practice being a grandma on them.

A special joy in preparing this book has been the valued assistance of Pamela Martin McCarville, whom I first knew when she was a student in my English class and the daughter of teaching colleagues. Her talent and insight have enhanced the experience of writing and have made beautiful all that she touches.

The poetry in this book was written over a long period of time and waited for years to be collected, organized and prepared for publication. But I finally did what I always told my students to do: I began.

Bette Milleson James is co-author of *Colorado Cravings* with Gail Riley and has been published in several anthologies of prose and poetry. Her work also appears in N. A. Noël's *I Am Wherever You Are,* a collection of poems and angel images for those who have lost a child.

Prologue:
The World's Children

The world's children are not ours,
though we love them,
(Or neglect to love them, as we sometimes do).
They belong to themselves and to God.
Ours is not to cause them pain or bring them sorrow.
Ours is to soothe the heart and guide the spirit,
To lead and protect each child,
And to save the very essence of the soul
From a world of vast confusion.
In this we must not fail.
Dream your dream for your own life,
But live your life for the world's children
And your own,
For they have a divinity in them,
And all of them are His.

Dedication

Bless the Children is dedicated to all the children of the world, who most need blessings, and to the parents and the many others who care for and bless them.

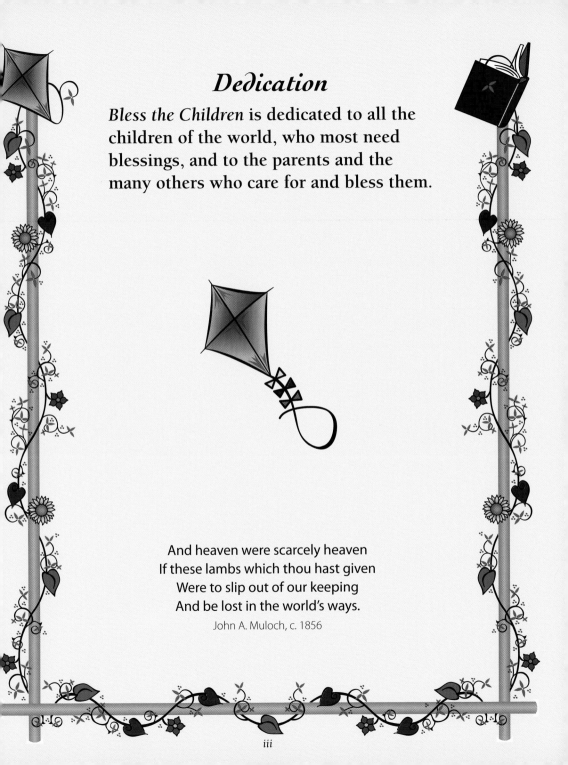

And heaven were scarcely heaven
If these lambs which thou hast given
Were to slip out of our keeping
And be lost in the world's ways.

John A. Muloch, c. 1856

Table of Contents

And Big Kids Too

For unto us a child is born,
unto us a son is given,
and the government shall be upon his shoulder,
and his name shall be called Wonderful, Counselor,
The Mighty God,
The Everlasting Father, The Prince of Peace.

Isaiah 9:6-7

One Child

Deep December:
A child sleeps, enfolded in family,
Love brought to Earth by God Himself,
While one star glows
And thrice-lived wisdom approaches,
Awestruck, bearing good gifts.
Love grows for us, it seems,
In this one child
In His own time.

Snows of Winter and warm Summer rains
Have come and gone.
Rushing Autumn leaves and early Spring blooms
Sweep on in flow unaltered,
Through hundreds and thousands of years,
And love still grows
One child at a time.

Thus, through eons and a universe,
Through all our little days of good or ill,
Love is brought to Earth again,
Again, and yet again.
And so, once more, in deep December,
A child sleeps, enfolded in family,
And love still grows
One child at a time.

Nearer the gate of paradise than we,
Our children breathe its airs, its angels see;
And when they pray, God hears their simple prayer,
Yea, even sheathes His sword, in judgment bare.

Richard Henry Stoddard, 1825-1903

Jack, by Night's Window

Midnight, and a billion stars
Crowd the sky outside your window.
Small and sleepless, too new to define them,
You lie in silence, mesmerized within your crib
Beside the darkened brilliant sky's lights,
Reflected in your eyes.
What do you know of them?
What do you remember of their purpose,
Their meaning,
Their eternal connection to your spirit?
You read those stars, hear them, recognize them.
Do they bring you the voice of God,
The words of His Archangels?
Or do they light the place you left behind,
And show the path to this one?

You are not like the rest of us, baby boy,
Not like other beings, not yet.
You live and breathe a planetary life's beginning,
But your eyes, your heart, your spirit
Touch the stars.

She is to live forever,
and will always wear the impress of my hand…
God has put the living material in my hand,
and I am to build an eternal destiny.

H. E. B., 1862, *Mother and Her Work*

Beneath the Tree
of Christmas

Beneath the tree, your infant eyes gaze upward,
Focused,
Light flowing into them
With the ultimate, most pure essence:
Knowledge of the glow above you
And the glow within you.

Tiny and new, you hold all else irrelevant
But the glow that fills your being
And holds your eyes fixed in purpose
To drinking in the light.

Thus, we see what we have lost,
And in your honored and beloved newness
Seek to find again
What once we saw in wonder,
As now we see in wonder
Your infant eyes gaze upward, beneath the tree.

Blessed be the hand that prepares a pleasure for a child,
for there is no saying when and where it may bloom forth.

Douglas Jerrold, 1803-1857

Baby Hands

Newest small one,
Deeply asleep upon your back
In the soft bend of your mother's arm,
You twitch slightly in your dreams and sigh deeply.
Two small hands rest loosely on your tummy,
Small fingers curved
Into dimpled and plumply soft fists.

Hands tell stories when we are old,
Stories about years of harsh labor
And life-scars whitened by time,
Or soft lives carefully attentive to gracious living,
About long lives of achievement and triumph
Hardly gained by untold effort
And sometimes by pain.

So, too, will your hands, sleepy baby,
In years yet unimagined
Tell of your life and its work,
Its harms, its many joys and exploits,
And the ultimate being at the core of all you have done.
You will make your mark upon a changing world
By your hands and how you use them,
According to your life with us and to our teachings,
With help from God, who sent you.

Children everywhere fly on the warm, sunny side of hope.

Jean Paul Friedrich Richter, 1763-1825

Infant in Flight:
Coming Home

Held aloft by technological marvels,
You sleep high above the earth all unaware,
Traveling to your new home in a new country.
Safeguarded by companions and attendants,
You come in an aircraft, its guided flight so routine
That the real wonder of it is lost to the confidence
That it will bring you here.

Your very life is held aloft, baby boy,
In your spiritual sleep, all unaware,
By the hand of your Maker
Who guides your soul in its lofty aspirations
And navigates the vast empyrean on your behalf,
And the real wonder of that, too, is lost to confidence
That He has brought you here.

Child, you are like a flower,
So sweet and pure and fair.

Heinrich Heine, 1797-1856

Jonathon at One Month

Tiny new wonder,
Center of our lives
And beginning of yours,
How do you see the world of your infancy?
How do you know,
In your new and unfocused consciousness,
That we are here for you?

Dreaming in perfect contentment,
In confidence and infant detachment,
Eyes moving under closed, feather-lashed lids,
You know a world complete in one warm room
Peopled by passionately devoted others
Who come and go throughout your days
With comfort and care for you alone.

Dream on now through infancy
And move then into childhood,
Through your centered awareness of self
Into clarity and knowledge of life with others.
Come out from your dream, little Jonathon.
You occupy our hearts already.

If there is anything that will endure
The eyes of God because it still is pure,
It is the spirit of a little child,
Fresh from His hand, and therefore undefiled.

Richard Henry Stoddard, 1825-1903

Sacred Infant

To plumb the depths of an infant's eyes
Is a thing not possible to do.
Measureless knowledge lies in those pools,
And remembrance of Heaven's cherished safety.

In these first weeks,
When your dark-eyed inward look
Is deep with undecipherable awareness,
A new little soul is visible,
Who remembers God and wisdom
And the last good-bye,
Who knows where he has come from,
And releases slowly and unwillingly the memory
Of the last farewell in Heaven.

Now you are in our care—
One of God's beloved souls,
Full of knowledge unavailable to us
Until, with gradual focus
Through eyes of indefinable color,
You finally begin to see us, and you smile
And become a part of our world:
A gift from God, a part of Heaven,
And a part of us as well.
You have all of this in common
With the Son of God Himself,
And you are ours.

How he sleepeth! Having drunken
Weary childhood's mandragore,
From his pretty eyes have sunken
Pleasures, to make room for more—
Sleeping near the withered nosegay,
which he pulled the day before.

Speak not! He is consecrated—
Breathe no breath across his eyes.
Lifted up and separated,
On the hand of God he lies,
In a sweetness beyond touching—
held in cloistral sanctities.

Elizabeth Barrett Browning, 1806-1861

Sweet, Sleepy Baby

With your innocent ways, you softened my spirit
And my life is not the same.
Ten small fingers touched the fringes of my heart,
Curled themselves around it
And took it from me forever.

What is home without a baby,
With each gentle, winning way,
Ever-glancing smiles inviting
Fond caresses all the day?

H. E. B., 1862, *Mother and Her Work*

Beautiful Child

Beautiful Child, how I love you!
Sleeping away the hours of night,
Wordless images of light and motion
Stirring in your gentle dreams,
You stretch when I lift you,
Secure, confident, safe.

Awake, you yawn and smile,
The dark pools of your eyes focusing on my face,
Inches away,
Unknowable knowledge within them,
Uncorrupted, incorruptible soul,
Neoteric innocence
Fresh from God.

I lift you to my shoulder,
Your soft form fitting into the curve of my neck,
And know that this is now my life:
To help you understand,
Beautiful Child, how I love you.

The soul is healed by being with children.

Fyodor Dostoyevsky, 1821-1881

You Live in My Heart

Ah, my small one
You live in my heart like a galaxy's bright star,
A diamond in the Milky Way,
A gleam of love galactic,
Brightest in the light-dimmed sweep of stars dusting
Across the universal sky.

These lines of heart,
Writ with quill from angel's wing
Upon the Vast of time and space,
Come from long-remembered days through innocence
Forever moving into knowledge
And change
To a point of brilliant awareness:
This alone will never change.
You live in my heart.

There are none of us who have stolen softly behind a child
when laboring in a sunny corner digging a Lilliputian well,
or fencing in a six-inch barnyard,
and listened to his soliloquies and his dialogues with some imaginary being,
without our hearts being touched by it.

Richard Henry Dana, 1815-1882

Miniature Memories

Miniature memories flood through my mind,
Flashes of joys and past heart string vibrations.
A smile, a touch, a little tug for attention—
A small hand 'round my finger, tight and trusting,
A quick, shy smile, a teasing eye,
A lock of curl on the nape of a neck,
A vulnerable vein, blue across a temple, fine and soft,
And all the children of my life roll into one,
Each newly come from God's own hand.

You touched the strings of my heart
And a chorded melody of many tones
Rang through my soul.
Now its echo fills my being:
Its euphony winds its way through every chamber of my soul,
And my spirit sings with tones immortal,
Vibrant music in concert with that of all mankind
With every mother's memory
Of every child.

Sweetly sleeping, you hold my heart,
And small though you are,
Your power is absolute,
Enriched as it is with both memory
And anticipation.

Ye are the children of light,
and the children of the day: we are not of the night,
nor of darkness.

I Thessalonians 5:5

Vulnerability

Long before this moment by the lighted tree,
The glowing, burnished gold of Christmas,
My heart knew many loves,
All preparation for these days,
For these years:
These eyes of unquestioning wonder,
Bright with many reflected lights;
These small lifted faces,
Warm and warming
In perfect acceptance
Of their own perfection.

Children of my child,
Creators of my newest love,
They are progenitors, too,
Of my latest vulnerability.
For who could have known
Of a new depth of joy,
And a new precariousness,
Together,
Before these years with children new,
Beside the trees of Christmas?

I love these little people;
and it is not a slight thing when they,
who are so fresh from God, love us.

Charles Dickens, 1812-1870

Higher

You sit precariously
On the bright plastic seat of a toddler swing,
Small fingers grasping the lifeline of yellow rope.
Higher! Higher!
What do you see?
What do you feel?
What do you know that I have forgotten?

Delighted squeals,
Laughing eyes,
Windblown curls:
These are all you are and all you want to be--
The present moment in a shining, golden ball of time.

Give me back again, then,
Your small and perfect world:
The higher view that shows another place,
The rising heart that skips a beat for joy,
The perfect truth that all you see
And feel
And know
Within your golden ball this moment
Is enough,
As you sit precariously
On the bright plastic seat of a toddler swing.

God sends children for another purpose than merely
to keep up the race – to enlarge our hearts;
and to make us unselfish and full of kindly sympathies and affections;
to give our souls higher aims;
to call out all our faculties to extended enterprise and exertion;
and to bring round our firesides bright faces, happy smiles,
and tender, loving hearts.
My soul blesses the great Father every day,
that He has gladdened the earth with little children.

Mary Howitt, 1799-1888

Overheard

"Jack!
Jack! You can't hit your sister.
Say sorry."
"No."
"Come over here.
One.
Two.
OK, go to time out."
(Wailing)
"Jack, I'm on the phone.
You have to stop crying so I can hear Grandma.
I need you to take a deep breath and stop crying.
Or go to your room. You choose."
"I can stop without a deep breath."
"OK, then stop."
(Wailing)
"Stop or go to your room."
(Sniffling, silence)
"OK, you can go out of time out now."
"I'm not ready yet."
"Then go when you're ready, OK?"
(Pause)
"OK. I'm going."
(Pause)
"Jack! You can't hit your sister!
Say sorry."
"No!"
"Come over here.
One…"
Repetition, it seems, is essential to learning.

Backward, turn backward, O Time, in your flight,
Make me a child again just for tonight!

Elizabeth Akers Allen, 1832-1911

Echoes of Voices:
Hanna

Beautiful Beloved Child,
The first of a new generation,
Cherished validation of all our lives,
Promised dream of all our futures,
And love of my own life,

You hold in your small hand
The strings of my heart,
And tug at them gently
With every echo of your mother's words
From long ago.
Words bring new life to old memories;
Repeated now, they strike new chords,
Harmonies of child-words,
In rhythmic echoes of old dreams,
Musical angel voices of then and now.

With every sweet response to life around you,
Each eager burst of joy,
Each gentle broken heart,
Each whispered melodic angel word,
You give back all the love I offer you,
And make me feel again
Echoes of love
For my own long-ago
Beautiful Beloved Child.

When the first baby laughed for the first time,
the laugh broke into a thousand pieces and they all went skipping about,
and that was the beginning of fairies.

J. M. Barrie, 1860-1937

Small Boy at Play

It is August,
And mottled sunshine sparkles on the water.
The backyard pool, filled by your father, is small,
But a wonder of water-jumping joy to you.
Grassy shade surrounds your play place,
Green and cool over wading-water.
Mottled sunshine ripples across your back
And sparkles in air-borne droplets.
Suddenly, you squeal
And splash your water at Daddy to scare him
As he passes with the mower,
And he gets you back
With a quick backstep and a tickle.
Your life rings often with belly-deep laughter,
For you are blessed with a father
Who is blessed with a sense of play.

Children are the keys of Paradise.
They alone are good and wise,
Because their thoughts, their very lives, are prayer.

Richard Henry Stoddard, 1825-1903

Adopting Udo

It was summer when you came to America,
Green and blue summer, a golden day in June.
The Colorado sky was clear,
And all your new family waited under the tented mountain-roof
Of Denver's giant airport.
So small, so sleepy,
Carried for so many hours by Aunt Jena
Aboard a long high flight from a far land,
You left behind the sounds of familiar language,
The sights and scents, the faces you knew.
You came to a new world of strange visions and voices,
Unfamiliar faces and unknown touch,
Leaving behind your ephemeral infant memories.

For months, new little boy, adopted by us all,
You were nearly silent,
Absorbing the new sounds of unfamiliar language,
The new surroundings and the gentle people who filled your life,
Wisely speaking only in smiles and small, rare cries.
Now you've grown and changed and have become a kindred spirit
Of happy disposition with your parents.
Now you walk and play and talk your toddler language.
Now you like stories and games and music and outdoors.
Now, little Udo, you have made a place for yourself
In the hearts and lives of family,
By bringing from a far land a certain joy and fulfillment.

Who is there whom bright and agreeable children
do not attract to play and creep and prattle with them?

Epictetus, A.D. c. 50- c.138

Bubble Rising

You blew bubbles in the yard today,
You and your big sister,
And one big, glistening, aurora-borealis globe of air
Caught your eye, and your ambition.
With the unquestioning confidence of childhood,
You reached grandly toward the sky with both hands wide,
Laughing as the bubble glided up and far away,
Driven by lightness and breezes
Into the incredible invisibility of light and shadow,
Untouchable, untouched, above you.
Its rising neither dampened your eager spirit,
Nor deterred your willing reach,
But only added to the fun of living in that moment.
Touch the bubble, and it would be gone,
But, ah, the glory of the reaching!

One day, little Maddie,
The bright bubble of your life's ambition
Will gleam like summer sunlight,
Surprising and inspiring you with new awareness
And with eager knowledge of what you can become.
And then, as you find yourself and your new life,
This same delighted confidence
And this magical joy in the reaching
For a new and cherished goal
Will send your touch beyond your grasp,
To chase the bubble of your heart's desire,
As you learn that the joy is in the journey
And not in journey's end.

A simple child,
That lightly draws its breath,
And feels its life in every limb,
What should it know of death?

William Wordsworth, 1770-1850

Night Child Vigil

Deep in the night,
You lie in restless sleep
Near a moonlit window,
Fevered, whimpering, helpless:
A child of patient, slow renewal,
Of prayer-answered, yet precarious health.

I feel the fear at unknown futures,
The sadness at your pain,
And dream of summer days in sunlight,
Laughing eyes
And windswept curls,
Days past and days to come.

Made vulnerable by love,
I sit near the window
Feeling the sorrow of child pain,
The fear of child loss,
The hope of child future,
As deep in the night
You lie in restless sleep.

I remember, I remember
How my childhood fleeted by, –
The mirth of its December
And the warmth of its July.

Winthrop Mackworth Praed, 1802-1839

Feeding the Horses

One day in summer,
You ran through the grass in absolute abandonment,
Incautious and joyous,
Playing pretend.
The little horses in the yard were hungry and thirsty.
You came three times to the front porch
To pick up handfuls of the hay of your imagination
And pretend pans of mustn't-spill-it water,
And the animals who breathed their life only for you
Had feasting beyond their painted concrete dreams.

With what endearing confidence and trust
You knew they would eat your hay!
With what eager steps and reckless joy
You ran down the grassy hill,
Curls and summer skirts bouncing in the sun,
Bare feet flying, tickled by the grass!
You called to your horses,
"Coming, coming!"
And they waited with the patience of statues.

How I loved you that day, Hanna,
For your quick step and wind-tossed hair,
Your laughter and friendly chatter,
Your eagerness to partake of life
And to offer yourself to it.
In your innocence, you found your joy
In that which does not exist.
It was a day when I saw again
That you are a light in the only sun I know,
And you carry that light with you,
Coming in and going out.

Child of the pure, unclouded brow
And dreaming eyes of wonder!

Lewis Carroll, 1832-1898

Hero

Little hero of the future
With Uncle Mark's vintage fire truck
Rolling across the carpet beside you,
Who will you become?
What will be your life's endeavor?
What will be your contribution,
As yet undreamed and unimagined?
We know only this:
Your true little soul, your strong young spirit
Are good already.
That bodes well for your future
And ours.

They are idols of hearts and households;
They are angels of God in disguise;
His sunlight still sleeps in their tresses;
His glory still gleams in their eyes.
Oh those truant from home and from heaven,
They have made me more manly and mild,
And I know how Jesus could liken
The kingdom of God to a child.

Charles Dickens, 1812-1870

Christmas Toddler

Secure in the bend of my arm,
Small fingers grasping my collar,
You lean to the tree of light,
And your eager eyes shine.
Enormous in your toddler face,
Timeless in their glow of faith and expectation,
They absorb the light of the Christmas Tree,
Giving back the shine with their own soft love,
Acceptance
And singular focus.

Beloved child,
Innocence adored of jaded experience,
Lend us your eyes,
Your faith, your expectation,
Your glow of love,
That we may find acceptance,
Absorbing within us the True Light
Of this Christ Mass -- the glow of singular focus --
The wordless wonder of the gift from God,
Secure in the bend of my arm.

He that raises a large family does, indeed, while he lives to observe them,
stand a broader mark for sorrow;
but then, he stands a broader mark for pleasure, too.

Benjamin Franklin, 1706-1790

Buddies at Christmas

Two little boys by the Christmas tree,
One with dark hair softly shining,
One with fair irrepressible curls,
Playing among the presents like the gifts from God they are,
Have bonded somehow, quickly,
Small cousins in sync with one another.
One is tiny, barely on "the chart,"
The other a big fellow, topping the standard.
Yet they are best buddies: The strapping boy
Guides the smaller as he toddles through the Christmas house,
The little one wandering in great curiosity
Through his buddy's domain.

Would that humanity could follow the children,
Whose purity of thought and action leave little room for conflict,
Whose small disagreements and tragedies are quickly forgotten,
Whose kinship with the Christmas Child is so close and intimate
That they seem one with Him, as truly,
In many ways, they are.

The smallest children are nearest to God,
as the smallest plants are nearest the sun.

Jean Paul Friedrich Richter, 1763-1825

Who is Sam?

Sammy, Sammy, who are you, really?
You look so calmly at the world,
So seriously in contemplation,
So observant, so measuring,
Then you burst suddenly into toddler laughter
Prompted by any sudden movement,
By a tumble, a noisy toy, a sound, a touch.
Little changeling, delight of our lives,
Your siblings treat you like a toy,
Hiding and finding, wrestling and rolling,
Teasing out your belly-laugh.

Wonderful, perfect little boy,
To your parents, you are a darling...
To your siblings, you are a playmate...
To all of us, you are a treasure.
To yourself...
Your own supremely confident, independent person!
Who are you, really?
In time, your very life will show us.
For now, you are silent contemplation...
And rollicking laughter unrestrained.

Children are living jewels dropped unsustained from Heaven.

Robert Pollock, 1799-1827

Little Boy Shopping

Little boy shopping with Mama...
Your bright smile and busy mind
Belie the circumstance we call your 'disability'
(Because we have no better word).
Your sparkling eyes miss nothing.
On the floor, you struggle
To keep up with your brother,
But struggle willingly, knowingly,
Persistently, successfully, full of joy.
Your future lies assured by your indomitable spirit,
Your eagerness, your curiosity,
Your bright, clear mind.
Though your small legs will not work properly,
A perfect little soul is shining from your eyes.

For where your treasure is, there will your heart be also.

Luke 12:34 and Matthew 6:21

Family Treasures

Children form the core of the values of a family.
In them resides the past, flowing from well-nourished roots
All firmly clinging to the soil of history.
In them resides the present,
full of joy and a disciplined, nurturing love
All intermingled among the several lives of family.
In them resides the future, the many unimagined facets
All waiting to become the lives that we must prepare them to live.

Through all these times, through our own past and theirs,
Through transitory now and our unknown, indefinable future,
The beings who really count are the children.
They are our love, our care, our nurturance, our treasures.
And where our treasure is, there our hearts are also.

A child is an angel dependent on man.

Count Joseph de Maistre, 1753-1821

Angelic Memory: Madalyn

Beautiful child of sparkling eyes
All the joys of eternity are in your laughter:
Echoes of angel elation,
Musical in this new existence,
Ring through time from other raptures
And delight our present moments with ancient mirth.
A part of universal love is shared
In your merry merging of spiritual and human existence.

Time is our memory's inhibition,
Causing our lost remembrance of the merging.
Great insulator of joy from original sources,
Hindrance to our faith
And to our knowledge of God,
Time, indeed, is too much with us.
Thus, eternity is lost to our own distance from it,
To too much of this sober moment
And too little of delight.

Now a day has come with sunlight
And vibrant green,
Filled with the infinite merriment of your life,
Singing with your laughter,
Rejoicing in your pleasure:
With you we can become again,
For a moment in time and in angelic memory,
A beautiful child of sparkling eyes,
Full of joy.

Beaning Star

The conversation went something like this:
"Mommy, how do you spell 'bright'?"
"b...r...i...g..."
"g ?"
"It's silent. And then there's a silent 'h'."
"OK. g...h..."
"What is the next letter, Hanna?"
"...t ?"
"Right!"

"Now, how do you spell 'beaning'?"
"Beaning?"
"Yes, you know, 'beaning'."
"What are you writing, Hanna?"
"Our new song. It's about a bright, beaning star."
"Oh! You mean 'beaming.' It's b...e...a...m..."
"Not beaming! bea-NING! A bright, be..."

"There isn't a word called 'beaning,' Sweetie.
Write 'beaming.' Stars beam."
"No. It's beaning. I listened very carefully, Mommy,
And learned the whole song.
A bright, beaning star.
How do you spell 'beaning'?"

"B...e...a...n...i...n...g."

How nice, we thought.
We have a sweet little pre-school girl
Who listens very carefully
And is always right.
In matters of auditory discrimination,
Her little five-year-old opinion
(For the time being)
Is law.

We hope she keeps forever, not the error,
But the absolute conviction
Of her mind.

We find delight in the beauty and happiness of children
that makes the heart too big for the body.

Ralph Waldo Emerson, 1803-1882

Give a little love to a child, and you get a great deal back.

John Ruskin, 1819-1900

Metamorphosis: Carmie

On a summer evening in the month of June,
A warm, begonia-scented, beach ball, back yard kind of evening
With cicadas singing in the trees
And a little girl of seven years to keep me company,
I sat on the red glider and thought of days gone by and days to come.

You were the little girl, and you brought with you a sun-kissed smile
And a sparkle of laughter. You madly chased a large blue ball
Down the green hillside under the silver maple tree,
And you sat for a moment on the brick wall
Above the lilac blossoms in your white and purple shirt,
Smiling for the camera, a flower among flowers.
I remembered then a colicky, weeping, inconsolable baby
Of three months' endless wailing
Who, in the middle of a sniffle, suddenly stopped crying
And has laughed every day since that metamorphosis of spirit.

What a blessing was that moment
When you found laughter to carry you through life,
Joy and confidence and the power of self
To grow and become your own person.
Child laughter and aged hope are somehow the same,
And so you have within you both joy and hope,
Both today and tomorrow, both child and woman,
Growing now and changing in the eighth year of your life,
On a warm, begonia-scented, beach ball, back yard kind of evening
In the month of June.

A child's life has no dates; it is free, silent, dateless.
A child's life ought to be a child's life, full of simplicity.

Oswald Chambers, 1874-1917

Snow Day

"It snowed last night!"
No better words could fill the quiet air of morning.
"It snowed last night!" and nothing is the same.
Outside the window, rounded creamy shapes hide reality
And soft swirls around the lamp post speak of gusty wind.
Too tempting, snow draws children out like magic,
Their cries shredding the silence,
Their boot prints and snow angels many, and deliberate,
Their snowman co-ops presenting giants
Among the snowmen of the world.

Cedar trees are buried under wide and drifted mountains,
And in them, a cave, a hollowed snow fort, a chilly hideaway.
Sliding without sleds, upside down, is the best of all games,
Slipping from the tops of snow-buried cedars
To roll tumbling to a stop in mounded white drifts.
Bright, warm coats and hats and mittens
Show with sunny brilliance the woolen colors of winter.
But even so—even so, the cold creeps in
And suddenly the noses won't unwrinkle,
The fingers in the mittens are nipped blue with frost,
The toes are feeling numb and uncommonly large.
But little matter: Euphoric with freedom from school's routine,
The running, playing, giggling, climbing,
Tunneling, tumbling children of winter play on,
Lost in the magic of four words, long wished-for:
"It snowed last night!"

We wove a web in childhood,
A web of sunny air.

Charlotte Brontë, 1816-1855

Prescient Moment: Kelsey

Today you came to my house
For a button-sorting day,
And we had lemonade
And conversation on the steps.
In your youthful blue-jean confidence,
You walked on the garden wall
Above the budding peonies
And lifted your arms and the tips of your fingers
Like feathered wings.
You moved lightly, taller than I had known,
And somehow older than I had noticed.
Strands of sun-blonde wind-whipped hair
Brushed across your face, softly--
Delicately balancing, you ignored them.
Rows of heavily blooming purple lilacs
And deep green cedar trees grew in lines behind you.
It was a very pretty picture,
And it is etched into my mind forever.
You laughed when you saw me watching,
And the blue of the sky expanded to glow in your eyes.
You are a child of joy and grace
And of healthy self-acceptance
At your proud new double-digit age of ten.
Yet in this prescient moment,
The woman you will one day be is here before my eyes:
Kind and proud, delicate and balanced,
Confident, true, and full of grace,
Walking lightly on the garden wall
And lifting her arms and fingertips
Like feathered wings.

Every child born into the world is a new thought of God,
an ever-fresh and radiant possibility.

Kate Douglas Wiggin, 1856-1923

Child of My Heart

Only you are you.
You are unique in all the world,
In all of space,
In all of time.
There is a place in the heart of my heart
That only you can fill.
Remember this truth,
For nothing will ever change it:
Only you are you.

Of all sights which can soften and humanize the heart of man,
there is none that ought so surely to reach it
as that of innocent children enjoying the happiness
which is their proper and natural portion.

Robert Southey, 1774-1843

Kite Children, With Ribbons

Born to rushing Kansas wind,
Children of the prairie rise to sunlight,
Lifted by generations of confidence
And truth.
Guided by long kite strings of parental care,
They reach in delight for Heaven's blue.
Winds that lift kites,
Breathless and gusty, without direction,
Give pause to loving hands that hold the strings.
Kite-tail ribbons whip and twist in windy skies,
Yearning for freedom.
We know the need,
Remember the anticipation.

And so we measure not only the joy of the kites,
But the strength of the kite strings
To hold them;
Not only the beauty of the bright, free ribbons,
But the power of the winds aloft
To take them.
High on ancient currents,
Blue kites and red ones fly free, yet bound by love.
Some show stripes and brilliant contrasts;
Some, uniquely indescribable, tug at lines with eager joy.
They know who they are.
And the careful hands know that they know.
But it is too soon, too soon, to let them go.

Winds of Change:
The Prairie

Ancient winds course lively over green-gold treeless plains,
The sounds of rushing gusts made musical
By warm air flowing through golden native grasses.
Black-haired children run in glee,
Their buckskin fringes tangled
By the very wind that they themselves create.
The free life, free forms of native wisdom
Follow the little winding shapes
Through a thousand years' games of chase and win.

Nineteenth-century winds lift loose hair
And long swaying skirts
Of women walking beside the wagons.
Canvas covers flap in the gusts
And grasses stir, bending in the wind,
Brushing then on the passing wheels.
Men, with their livestock, their guns,
Their plows and their determination
Face the hot air rushing swiftly, unimpeded,
Across those same green-gold treeless plains.
Timeless winds and gusty air underlie all events,
Stir sounds in the night,
Carry the smoke from morning fires,
And follow among the joyous children as they run.

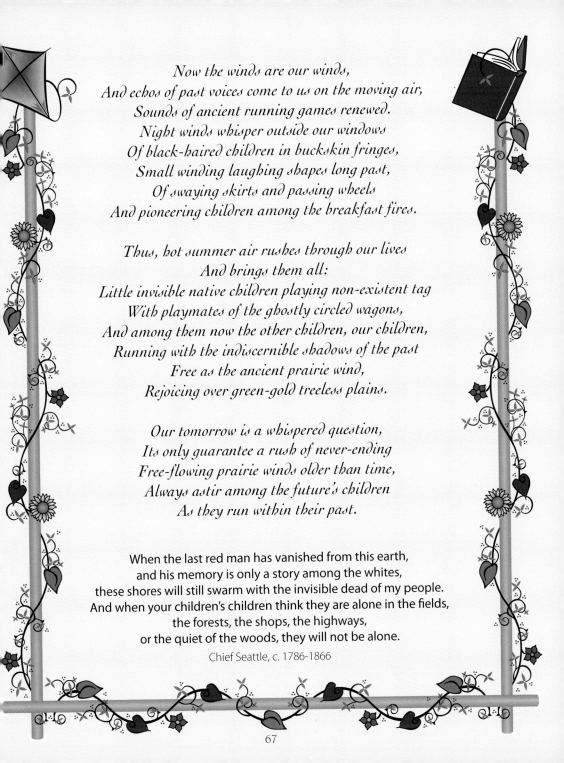

Now the winds are our winds,
And echos of past voices come to us on the moving air,
Sounds of ancient running games renewed.
Night winds whisper outside our windows
Of black-haired children in buckskin fringes,
Small winding laughing shapes long past,
Of swaying skirts and passing wheels
And pioneering children among the breakfast fires.

Thus, hot summer air rushes through our lives
And brings them all:
Little invisible native children playing non-existent tag
With playmates of the ghostly circled wagons,
And among them now the other children, our children,
Running with the indiscernible shadows of the past
Free as the ancient prairie wind,
Rejoicing over green-gold treeless plains.

Our tomorrow is a whispered question,
Its only guarantee a rush of never-ending
Free-flowing prairie winds older than time,
Always astir among the future's children
As they run within their past.

When the last red man has vanished from this earth,
and his memory is only a story among the whites,
these shores will still swarm with the invisible dead of my people.
And when your children's children think they are alone in the fields,
the forests, the shops, the highways,
or the quiet of the woods, they will not be alone.

Chief Seattle, c. 1786-1866

Ah! What would the world be to us,
If the children were no more?
We should dread the desert behind us
Worse than the dark before.

Henry Wadsworth Longfellow, 1807-1882

Epilogue:
Miracle

Beautiful, innocent, lucent miracle,
You are a gift to the world and a light to the future,
As all of the world's children are.
Give us your hand and your small new spirit,
Little child of light,
And follow us to truth.
Let us be your guides and teachers,
And we will lead and love you,
For you are the purpose of God and the universe,
Beautiful, innocent miracle.

Index of Classic Authors

Biblical Sources